383 7673

A Story About Believing In Yourself

(The new Little One edition)
© 2019 by Morty Sosland

Written by Ducktor Morty Sosland, M.D.
Illustrated by Sarah Sosland

Based on the original book illustrated by
Sarah Sosland, Arielle Sosland,
and Esther Deblinger, Ph.D.

Can Do Duck Publishing
PO Box 1045
Voorhees, NJ 08043

ISBN 978-0-9768384-4-9

For more information on this book
and other books in the Can Do Duck series,
please visit TheCanDoDuck.com

This is the tail of a baby duck.

"Welcome! Welcome everyone!
You're about to have some fun."
Mama Duck went on to say,
"You will learn to walk today!"

One duck was scared to walk or run.
And that duck was called Little One.
Little One hadn't walked before
and did not know what feet were for.
"Mama, I don't think I can.
I don't think you understand."

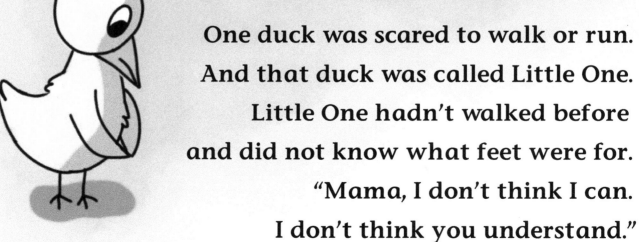

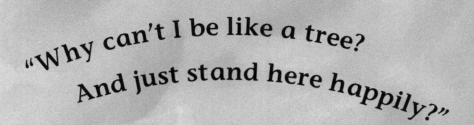

"Why can't I be like a tree?
And just stand here happily?"

But Mama said, "You're not a tree,
because you could not talk to me.
If you try, then you will see
just how great you can be!"

"First say, I can.

Then make a plan.

Get right to it.

And then you'll do it!"

"Imagine how you're gonna start,
how you'll do the hardest part,
how you'll feel when you're all done.
You'll think it was really fun!"

Little One said, "Yes, I can!

Now I'm going to make a plan.

I will walk just like my mother.

First one foot and then the other."

Mama Duck said, "Okay, folks,
now we'll learn some swimming strokes."
But getting wet did not seem fun.
Floating was hard for Little One.

"A pigeon does not have to swim,
Why can't I be just like him?"

"You're not a pigeon," said Mama Duck.
"And that means that you're in luck!
A pigeon's life I would not choose,
standing up on old statues!"

"The more you swim the more you'll see,

just how fun swimming can be."

"Imagine you are swimming fast

and that all your fear has passed.

You learned to walk and then you ran.

You can swim. Just say, I can!"

"I say **I can**.

I make a plan.

I get right to it.

And then I do it!"

Mama pointed to the sky.

"Now, my ducklings, we will fly."

"A cow does not have to fly,
Tell me, Mama, why do I?"

"I am glad that cows can't fly.
I don't want milk in my eye."

Little One laughed and agreed.
"I will fly now. Yes, indeed!"

Little One wasn't too scared
and was feeling quite prepared.
"I will imagine I'm up high
and I'm flying across the sky!"

Little One jumped in the air...

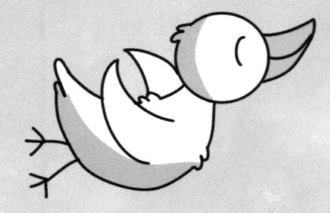

But then fell down with a scare.

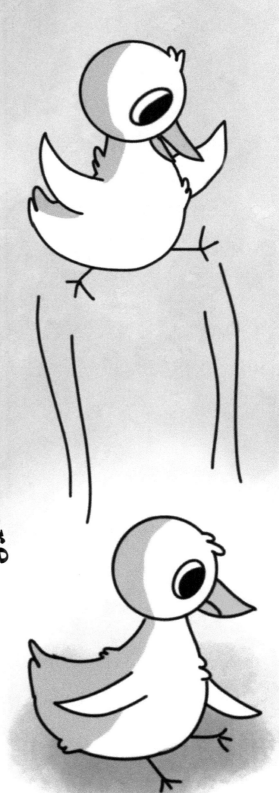

And what do you think happened then?
Little One just tried again!

I say **I can.** I make a plan. I get right to it. And then I do it!

Mama Duck was watching this.
She gave Little One a kiss.

"Oh look at how you have grown.
You can do things on your own.
You can fly and swim and run.
What have you learned my Little One?"

"I say **I can.**

I make a plan.

I get right to it.

And then I do it!"

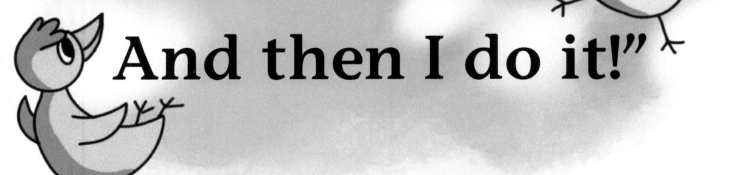

Some ducks might have had enough,
but Little One kept learning stuff.

Horseback riding,

rollerblading,

bowling,

golf,

and ice-skating!

They stared and pointed on the courts.
They never saw a duck in shorts!
By practicing every day,
Little One learned how to play.

Little One did much indeed
and even learned how to read,
in English, French and ancient Greek.
This wasn't easy with a beak.

Every day learning something new,
they started calling Little One **Can Do!**

The ducks thought Can Do was a star
and could do everything so far...

But then one day even Can Do
found something Can Do could not do.

Can Do could not fly at night.

Something just did not seem right.

In the dark you can't see trees.

You've got to watch your wings and knees.

Then Mama gave Can Do a kiss
and she said, "Now remember this.
I love you for being you.
Not because of what you do."

"When something is hard for you,
remember the things you can do!
You can do things in your own way
and you can practice every day."

Can Do set new sights so high.
"Whatever it is, I will try!"

"I will fly around the stars.
I'll be the first duck on Mars!
Will I get there? I don't know!
But I will work to make it so."

"I would not be hesitant
to even be the president."

"I'd teach you that you can do
what you put your mind to.
And then what else will I do?
I do not know. What would you?"

Imagine what you can do too.
You can do it like Can Do!
Go ahead. Say it with me.
Say it loud. It works you'll see...

"I say **I can.**

I make a plan.

I get right to it.

And then I do it!"

This story's ending for **Can Do**
but it's starting now for you.
Spread your wings. Get set to soar!
That's what saying **I can** is for!

The End or
The Beginning

Teacher and Parent Guidelines for The Can Do Duck

The Can Do Duck is not an ordinary duck and this is also not an ordinary story. It is a story of a duck that learns to overcome its fears and learns a process by which to achieve new goals. The story is meant to entertain and teach at the same time.

The story stresses the importance of positive self-talk. All of us talk to ourselves or think to ourselves hundreds, if not thousands, of times, every day which greatly influences our feelings and behaviors. Where negative self-talk can lead to anxious and distressed feelings, positive self-talk can help children and adults feel brave and optimistic. Moreover, positive self-talk can help children and adults to have the confidence to try new things and accomplish their goals. As Henry Ford said, "Whether you think that you can, or that you can't, you are usually right." In this story, with the help of Mama Duck, Can Do learns to talk and think about things in encouraging, positive ways. You will note in this new edition we do not refer to Can Do as a male or female duck so it's easier for boys and girls to relate to Can Do and become Can Do Ducks themselves.

There are many helpful lessons throughout the story. These include teaching children to believe in themselves and try new things. Can Do's experiences also highlight the importance of planning ahead and the story demonstrates that small successes can lead to greater successes. Can Do models for the reader how to break difficult tasks into small parts and also demonstrates how to visualize or imagine yourself getting through difficult tasks. Throughout the story, Mama Duck models the kind, positive encouragement that parents and teachers can offer when children are trying new things. Mama Duck conveys the importance of unconditional positive love, expressing perhaps the most important message children need to hear and feel: "I love you for being you. Not because of what you do."

A special note to parents about reading:

Modeling enthusiasm for reading can significantly motivate a child's interest in reading. You can demonstrate being enthusiastic by

1. reading out loud to a child (especially with a creative, theatrical flair)
2. listening to a child read, expressing interest, and offering lots of praise
3. reading a book, newspaper or magazine as your child reads silently alongside of you while you snuggle together on a couch
4. demonstrating your own interest in reading by having books, magazines, and other reading materials in the home.

Reading is like any other new activity a child is learning. It takes patience, repetition, practice, and gentle but persistent encouragement from a caring parent, teacher, or other adult.

Reading together also provides opportunities to talk with your child about experiences that they may have had that are similar to those experienced by the characters in the story. In The Can Do Duck, Can Do first acknowledged fears, shared them with Mama Duck and overcame them to achieve many goals. By starting a conversation about the story, a parent or teacher can begin to learn about what's on their child's mind.

The guidelines that follow can be helpful to parents reading with one child as well as teachers and principals who want to encourage Can Do attitudes among the students in classrooms and even throughout the school. We hope you will find some of the ideas useful in engaging students to believe in themselves and pursue their goals even when they feel unsure or scared.

1. Start with a general discussion about what the children liked the most about the story. Ask the children to summarize what happened in the story. What did they learn? What were their favorite parts? What did they think of Can Do? What did they think about Mama Duck? How are they like Can Do? Who gives them advice and helps them learn new things?

2. Ask the children what was the message of The Can Do Duck? What did Can Do learn?

3. Ask the children if they remember what Can Do repeats to do things even when Can Do is not sure if they can be done.

> I say I can.
> I make a plan.
> I get right to it.
> And then I do it!

Have them write it on the board or on a piece of paper so they can keep it in a pocket, desk or other special place. Ask the children what each line means. Have the children repeat the lines. Ask them if they know what a plan is? A plan is thinking how you will do something or planning what you will do later.

Ask the children what plans they have made before. They might (or their parents might) make plans to get together with a friend or make plans for a vacation. We can also make plans for how we will do something new. Ask the children, why it's important to get right to it?

4. In the story, Can Do learns to imagine doing something before actually doing it. This helps accomplish it.

> Imagine how you're gonna start,
> how you'll do the hardest part,
> how you'll feel when you're all done.
> You'll think it was really fun!

Ask the children to imagine themselves accomplishing something difficult.

5. Ask the children for examples of things that they used to not be able to do (or they were a bit scared to do) and how they were able to do it? (ex: learning how to ride a bicycle, learning to swim, learning to read, learning how to play a musical instrument, learning how to play a sport, etc.) You might give them an example of something that you did as a child or as an adult? (like becoming a teacher or learning a new skill) Ask them how they are like Can Do? How are they Can Do Kids?

6. Ask them for ideas of things that they are not sure they can do and that they would like to learn or do now if they could be like Can Do. What are some steps in a plan that they could think of to help them do it? Who could help them with that plan? (Their parent, relative, teacher?) Ask them for some ideas of things that they would like to learn or do in the future when they are grownups.

7. Talk about the fact that the Can Do Duck books were written by a father and the new color drawings were done by his daughter. She drew the color drawings as an adult but she and her sister drew the original black and white drawings when they were just 6 and 8. Would they like to write or draw pictures in a book of their own? What would their book be about? As an activity, the children could start working on their own books. They could first think of a character and then think of the story. Here are some of the original pictures. To see more, please go to the website, TheCanDoDuck.com

8. Recently, schools have been coming up with some creative ideas on how to use the Can Do Duck books. They have been giving out rubber ducks to students and teachers who demonstrate positive, Can Do attitudes. They've also given out other kinds of duck souvenirs to help children remember Can Do's message. One school has a large rubber duck and a note pad that travel from classroom to classroom. Each class writes on the note pad examples of things they've done with Can Do attitudes. Another school asked the children to draw pictures of goals they have for the future. They also write the Can Do message on top of their drawings. One high school volleyball team attached the Can Do slogan to the net while they practiced. Another school had the cheerleaders make a cheer using the Can Do message: We say we can. We make a plan. We get right to it. And then we do it! These are just a few ideas of ways that parents, teachers and schools have been using the Can Do Duck books. If you have other ideas, please share them with us so we can spread the word.

We hope that this book will inspire children and adults on their own Can Do journeys. You can do it like Can Do!

Sincerely yours,

Esther Deblinger, Ph.D.

Ducktor Morty Sosland, M.D.   DucktorMorty@TheCanDoDuck.com